Forest of Light

Poetry and Images on Nature and Life

Courtney L. Smith

First paperback edition August 2021

Cover design, Layout, Photography
and Editing by Courtney L. Smith

AUG 1 6 2021

For my daughters- my greatest creations.

I love you

I love you

I love you

Contents

Preface 6

Star Dance 8

Heart of Ancient Stone 11

A Wood Path 14

The Elders 16

I Met a Flower 20

The Faerie Woods 23

The Sky- From the Mat 27

In a Ghosted Wood 30

Enchanted Morn 34

Dear August 37

My Girls 40

Patchwork Bird 43

Yoga 46

Eagle 49

Half Dome 52

Forest of Light 55

Pastel Sky 58

Youth 61

Autumn 64

Forest of Light II 67

Mornings   70

A River Flowing   73

Darkness   75

Library   78

Lakeside   82

Siren   85

Symphony of the Sea   90

Wake up   93

The Spider   97

Nature's Song   100

Thunder   103

About the author   105

Preface

In this collection of poetry and images I honor the beauty of nature and life around and within us. I hope to bring you on a journey through seasons, forest wanderings, adventures, and reflections on my own life and photos of this beautiful world we live in.
As a writer and photographer, it's always been my intention to inspire the receiver or viewer of my art-to look a little deeper, find the extraordinary in the ordinary, and to savor everyday moments. Life around us is bursting with miracles from birdsong to trees communicating under the forest floor.

To study the life around our life is to become aware of the intricate eco-system we are a part of. With most people around the world living in metropolitan areas, there is a disconnect that occurs, either over time or from birth. Some people have never seen the stars in their full glory! Some have never seen the ocean or the mountains and some are scared of these things because they're the "unknown".

In Forest of Light, I hope to spark a light inside of you that finds you pausing to hear birdsong or reveling in the way the morning or evening light glitters and dances on the walls in your home.

I can tell you, I have an entire archive of tree

silhouettes dancing on the walls of my home in that perfect golden light.

Never pass up a chance to be curious, to pause, to enjoy being here in this moment. Just the fact that you exist to experience this incredible world is a miracle.

When I stand before trees thousands of years old, knowing they've seen the progress of humans and our destruction- it's humbling. Our lives are so short compared to these incredible, massive giants. It's an honor to share this space in time with them and with you. We are here for only one wild ride- let's make the most of it.

Star Dance

Evening light dissolves
trees become silhouettes
every leaf etched into the sky
I sit in the twilight
book in hand
between words my gaze wanders
through the trees
into the wide open stage
one star ablaze
It appears to dance
as if dangling on a string
tethered from space
it was just us
the star and I
I wonder how it could be
if I could fly
leaving the world behind
and travel through the sky
joining the stellar dance
for just one night

Defrosting bodies
Find their way toward the sun
Life begins again

Heart of Ancient Stone

I tumbled through aquatic vines
ride currents through lengths of time
plunged under colossal waves
to reach earth's elusive shrine

Sage hearts of an archaic world
worn smooth into woeful stone
the sun has risen many times
before these treasured shores I roam

I faintly breathe under the foam
flowing with the lunar tide
eyes above on the night sky
where the fiery stars collide

I watch a world where I begin
and one day will return
high above this forsaken land
after lessons have been learned

Rain melts into soil
Dormant energy expands
Fertile land once more

A Wood Path

Into the dampened woods
fresh from morning dew
life gently stirs
who is passing through

echos of elder pines
creaking in the breeze
ravens crow overhead
as kestrels dance with bees

weaving down the path
I hear a song under some leaves
a delicate little voice
inviting me to my knees

hidden in the overgrowth
the source is hard to see
but soon I am aware
who I'm searching for is me

The Elders

Tapping on your delicate bark
I venture to awaken
the elder within this ancient being
to share of moments when

when the deer ate from your limbs
and the birds pecked a hole
tell me of the greatest storm
a tale that's never been told

When did you reach most for the sun
as it tickled the top of your crown
have you held the weight of a comrade
or a nest filled with feathery down

When has your coat shed
to release a nourishing sap
to feed the world around you
as they rest upon your lap

When did the underground
feed your delicate wooden veins
and when did you wash your soul
with the hope of heavenly rains

Oh, tell me what's it's like to be
the eldest soul of this land
how to soothe the weary heart
while remaining steadfast and grand

Bumblebees grazing
Tulips stretch toward cloud patched skies
Picnics in the park

I Met a Flower

I met a flower yesterday
petals soft and pure
scented of the sweetest nectar
first blossom of the year

Balmy from the morning dew
my hands are damp with gold
a luxurious salve flows over
saving me from the cold

Suddenly, I'm overtaken
by radiant yellow light
this petite flower in my hand
has made me feel alright

A full worm moon rises
Buds appear on brittle bones
Heart beats grow faster

The Faerie Woods

As the final leaves descend
slowly to the earthen floor
I gather my belongings
and trek across the moor

A wintry chill arrives
traveling through the air
great winds stir
whirling through my hair

Mulling over the fables told
and memorizing lore
spoken by the elders
down near the shore

Entering my bitter cottage
I seal the windows and door
to settle into winter
and build fire to restore

Nestled near the flickering flames
with a pad and pen
I write of the faerie woods
should we meet again

Birdsong in the wind
Life carries on despite us
Light filters through pines

The romance of life
Is found in every flower
And the eyes who see it

The Sky - From the Mat

An azure afterglow
drifting into a deep sleep
silhouettes of branches
swaying to the hymns
within my ears
as if we are connected
a rhythm of universal truth
on repeat night after night
I sigh and the winds drift
through the leaves
a dance of elements
from one body to the next
a relay of life
on this cool summer night

Walking through the field
Heaven is a realm on earth
Flowers brush my legs

In a Ghosted Wood

As I traveled through the forest
a strange thing came to sight
amongst the greatest evergreens
arose a faint bright light

I looked around as though a fog
rolled in over me
but what appeared were ghostly trees
all along the stream

Slowly as I walked near
I tried to grasp the wood
it was then, in this moment
that I understood

Towering before me
were the trees of history
outstretching their limbs
to cast their noble memories

overhead I saw the lives
of every ancestral pine
who once ruled the land
several at a time

As though the sky a movie screen
of a world filled with trees
they wept for days gone by
as I settled beneath their leaves

A heavy mist began to fall
throughout the faded wood
I whispered a promise to keep them alive
as long as I could

Slowly the outline of the giants
began to vanish away
it was in the solemn moment
that I'd never be the same

Sun rays drench my face
Crashing waves blanket the shore
Summer's here at last

Enchanted Morn

Risen are the early birds
and those who cannot sleep
for thoughts swirl around
a river running deep

Tiptoe down the darkened hall
a dappled light ahead
chilled windowpanes frost
the orange glow has spread

Morning welcomes ravens
cawing out of doors
looking for a catch
wings spread, he soars

Enchanting is this time of day
when humans are still asleep
for me, I thrive with the wild ones
and the secrets that we keep

Dandelion clock
You take to the western wind
As the skies turn pink

Dear August,

It was a summer in which the sand felt just one degree too hot. We were on the precipice of imminent demise, but I stood watching you arrive. Your golden flames burst through the sky, clouds set alight.
We dug our toes to cooler sands and dove into the briny tide.
I drank ocean water - gulped it in fact. All I could taste was salt for the rest of the night. My hair dried into spires reaching toward your light.
I dreamed the dreams so many times that rest on this shoreline. For when we reunite I feel like a starseed blazing to paradise.
Beside this opulent ocean where we meet again- the water's fine, it's our time to shine, and we all move in slow motion.

x

Thick air settles in
The sky rumbles with wild light
We run for cover

My Girls

There is only one vital trait
I wish to pass along-
to marvel in the wild world
and the fervor to hear her song

Day after day I spent
pointing to the sky
"Look at the moon" I'd say
as it reflected in your eyes

Tucking scented flowers
neatly behind your ears
citing the names and notes of each
and how each one appears

Hoping my delight in all
the magic found outside
would carry on into your hearts
and be your loving guide

My hope is that many years from now
when you're amongst the tides or trees
you might sense a trace of my love
for you in every breeze

Sweltry heat lingers
We dip into the river
Gilded skies ignite

Patchwork Bird

I saw the most beautiful
average looking bird
his back- a patchwork of feathers
every earthen color woven
blending into each other
a tapestry of brown, black, and gold-
his cape for the wild skies
he sails through life so dazzling
yet never seen with his own eyes

Maps of old dirt roads
California's golden hills
Endless horizon

Yoga

Silence
go in
chest expands
ribs

Air flows through
expansion
lungs fill
blossom
open

Hush
out flows the breath
blocked energy within
exhale
to free the body
to begin again

to begin again

Majesty of waves
Surging under my body
Carried out to sea

Eagle

The campfire smoke billows
seducing the alpine breeze
dancing into muted light
as the moon filters through wavering trees

A stir in the wild flames
as golden embers charge the skies
I slowly rise to behold
a majestic form materialize

Feathered wings span several feet
an ivory gaze envelops me
the eagle grasps onto my back
revealing what I could not see

My spirit soars into the night
at last it is so clear
I have always been this free
underneath the idle fear

Riverside campsite
Sweet blackberry stained fingers
Chopped cedar in flames

Half Dome

Her wild beauty rises
far above the grassy plain
granite face shimmering
when even soaked in rain

There she stands- the jewel
of this treasured mountain range
an eternal life of stillness
and divinity in her veins

Flowing through the rivers
and every path through pine
her sacred mass casts
a spell on me every time

As time passes by
Leaves fall, vanish, and return
August here at last

Forest of Light

The dusty trail was dappled
with a thousand specks of light
each filtered through the leaves
settling everywhere in sight

The heavens sprinkled down
coins of vibrant gold
to be found by the wanderer
of this sacred path untold

To collect the treasure found
within this wooded land
one must open their heart
and disregard the hand

The forest of light can mesmerize
any roving soul
but only those with gratitude
will fill their bucket full

Dreams rise in spring skies
Later fall as memories
Etched in autumn leaves

Pastel Sky

Under the pastel sky
is where I feel most at home
wide open spaces
where all my thoughts can roam
I watch them dance around
putting on a show
so I can collect them one by one
then let them all go
free to the wind
I empty out my mind
this way I can explore
and see what I find
cleansing my spirit
the sky knows the way
I let the silver moon
rinse my woes away

Golden brown and rust
Leaves fall from every tree
Validating pause

Youth

I find myself slipping
between the space
of youth and some other place

A valley with views of either side
rivers and lakes
and tree lined skies

I wave goodbye to the rocky hills
and to the softness of a girl so young
while honoring her wishes as I go on

Soon I will reach the mountain peak
to take in the expansive view
a little weathered- but that's beautiful too

Soft rain on rooftops
Steady as nature's heartbeat
to soothe the weary

Autumn

The morning roused
as the sun flushed
a pale lit sky
tangerine hues
turn burnt sienna
a commencement of
crisp leaves drift by
ambling down the sidewalk
summers air turned brisk
seasons shift to rest
and release into
a golden bliss
of autumnal tonic
that glides in smooth
to regale worn senses
tailing harvest's moon
burrow into mild nests
glowing with candlelight
as the totality of life
settles in for the night

Nestled in dry leaves
Pine smoke billows from chimneys
Sky an orange hue

Forest of Light II

As dusk drifts into darkness
lights flick on across the bay
casting beams into the water
in a remarkable way

I sit on the floating dock
feeling it sway with the tide
and notice this other place
that daylight tends to hide

The vivid beams radiate
like stilts to an underworld
somewhere woven in the depths
a forest of light unfolds

I dip my toes into icy blackness
hypnotized by this sight below
stars increase overhead
I wonder if they know

This veiled world that appears
under the night sky
all just out of grasp
to the passerby

Crows fly westward
As silhouettes on coral skies
Fading into night

Mornings

I rise before dawn
stars still gleam through
the windowpanes
softened by a haze
to join in my salutations

Life feels palpable
in these early hours
of tender solitude

Morning- the marrow
of the day
rich in minerals
I mine with my
breath

Children in costumes
Caramel coated apples
Bags filled with candy

A River Flowing

I came across a river
flowing
deep within the woods

Rapids rushing, I felt it
knowing
wisdom of life and love

I sat and watched the water
rising
to meet me where I stood

Naturally, it was somewhat
surprising
to hear the roaring words

I leaned into the current
slowing
to listen to the song

She said-

Don't stop hoping in the
growing
of hearts that seem far gone

Scarlet leaves falling
Pockets filled with candy corn
Sipping on cider

Darkness

Darkness can mean
many things-
cover from the light
a state of being
a place worth seeing
or enchanter of the night

Darkness can mean
many things-
one's reason to stay inside
a haunting body
a hidden alley
or the depths of ocean tide

Darkness can mean
many things-
somewhere to explore
a time of day
a mood we stay
or the master of the stars

Golden harvest moon
Pine logs ablaze behind glass
Nesting in blankets

Library

My body is a library
every scar and bone
carved in memories

life and loss
love and laughter

A catalog of summers
pages of winter strewn

messes and miracles
mothering and madness

records of time
well spent and wasted

adventures and ailments
achievements and adversity

My body is a time capsule
of everything I've seen
everywhere I've been

creation and challenges
celebrations and chaos

An archive of autumns
springs tucked away

as each year passes
the collection expands
and while my library
fills to the brim
the memories start to fade

like vanishing ink
upon my brain

Breath on frosted glass
Flawless blanket of crystals
On the matted lawn

Lakeside

It was a balmy summer night
on the bank of a reposing lake
vivid stars thread into a duvet of clouds
heavy with temperate rain
drops slipping down sheer panels
of the tent that veils me
from this rapturous release
rinsing the earth
I feel the aura of life
in the lucent humidity
cooling air mingles with breath
I inhale heavily
it fills my lungs like
another body
stretching wings of dreams
I feel alive
oh my
I feel alive

Chestnuts over fire
People tucked into lodges
Refuge from the cold

Siren

Out to see the sailor cries
gripped in sirens song
hymns of otherworldly promises
lure him to the strand
ships collide with rugged bluffs
like supernovas in the sky
a magnificent display of light
shattered on the open sea
as he floats to his destiny
in the clutches of her wings

Snow covered rooftops
Merry markets in the square
Children writing lists

Spring
Came
And so did you
Rising to the top
Layers of my life
Everything else falls
To rest in your shadow
Too hard to compete

Symphony of the Sea

Sat on the cliff's edge
I thought I was alone
not a soul upon the stretch of beach
but I turned to see the moon
he sat just over my shoulder
to share this view with me
as the gale winds drew the storm
in from the raging sea

I watched as he cast
his reflection on the waves
he played with light and shadows
garnishing the water with glaze
as raindrops began to fall
along the incandescent sea
rhythms of earth and sky
became a grand symphony

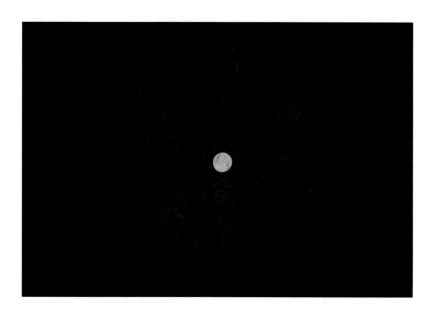

Freshly fallen snow
Marshmallows held over fire
Wet clothes strung nearby

Wake Up

I wonder what they think of us
these trees of millennium
watching us destroy ourselves
meddling with creation
we stir up dust in our short lives
to announce that we are here
causing the world we know
to slowly disappear-
maybe virtue lies
in every step untaken
preserving nature's elements
it's time we must awaken

Gentle soul- you embody
All the stars wrapped up
In a bow
A gift of light to this weary world

Farms of evergreens
To be chopped down one by one
And bestowed with light

The Spider

Eventide
the sky dims
silhouettes of
spiders spin
invisible webs
backlit by stars
shining silk stretched
near and far
to build his house
of dreams
a hammock
capturing moonbeams
in each thread
a divine light
to cradle his body
through the night

Twinkle lights on eaves
Festive songs dance through air waves
Hot mugs warming hands

Nature's Song

You can find the music of trees
in the space between the leaves
the winds dance on the ivories
with a sentient kind of ease

There's a pause within the breeze
when you can hear it easily
a seasoned harmony
of the love in everything

Snow falls in silence
Street lights illuminate flakes
Whiteout by midnight

Thunder

The thunder cracked
to let us know
we were still alive
pulsing through
the chambers
of our hearts

Racing like lightning
spiraling through veins
connecting us to
the elements
of the world
in which we
are the same

About the author

Courtney L. Smith is a writer, poet, photographer, calligrapher, yogi, nature lover, and mother living in Southern California.
She spends her time raising her beautiful daughters with her husband, hiking, reading, reflecting on her yoga mat, and capturing the world in her lens.
You can find her blogging in the wee hours of the morn at her little corner of the internet, clsmithwriter.com.